Ordinary Nagas

With Exceptional Stories

"A Collection of Short Stories"

Neon Phom

Copyright © 2016. All rights reserved.

No part of this publication may be reproduced, stored in a retrieval system or transmitted in any way by any means, electronic, mechanical, photocopy, recording or otherwise, without the prior permission of the author except as provided by USA copyright law.

All characters appearing in this work are fictitious. Any resemblance to real persons, living or dead, is purely coincidental.

The opinions expressed by the author are not necessarily those of Revival Waves of Glory Books & Publishing.

Published by Revival Waves of Glory Books & Publishing

PO Box 596 | Litchfield, Illinois 62056 USA

www.revivalwavesofgloryministries.com

Revival Waves of Glory Books & Publishing is committed to excellence in the publishing industry.

Book design Copyright © 2016 by Revival Waves of Glory Books & Publishing. All rights reserved.

Published in the United States of America

Paperback: 978-1-68411-185-5

"Be sober, be vigilant; because your adversary the devil, as a roaring lion, walketh about, seeking whom he may devour."

1 Peter 5:8

Dedicated to my mother

Abeni Phom

Preface

Why this book? All the narrations are based on true stories of ordinary people with extra ordinary faith and belief in God. You don't have to baffle on the thought of being misguided. Many Christians are not practical people; they know how to bait the hook, but they themselves don't practice what they preach. It's the antipode of who they really are. This book will help you realize that there are thousands of people in the world facing the same problems as you and trying to survive despite the harsh realities in life. I have not used the real names of the characters in the stories I have written. The stories in this book are about people who took struggle as a challenge rather than a failure.

Message

Most of us give up so easily when we face failures and we only see obstacles and worry about what is yet to come. Do not worry for your tomorrow because God is always with you. Through the stories I have written, my purport is not to blight the reader's mindset but to convey a very simple message. It takes confidence and maturity to face failures. Never let anyone look down on you nor patronize you but you be an example in faith, love and purity. Don't give up just yet because you don't know what plans God has for you. There is no canon on how to live a contented life but it's a skill to stay contented.

Do not let failures be your weakness because your weakness is like your master. It is like a person imposing authority on you and it will control your mind and your way of thinking. Fear is the reason the weak cannot move on. Moving on with your life despite failures will make you more confident and consolidated in faith.

Yes, failure is the reason why many people give up without knowing the fact that failure is just the way of saying you still have to try the other way. Do not waste your precious God gifted blessed life on earth regretting.

There is no clog or obstacles that will slow you down if you trust in the Lord with all your heart and he will direct your path. Nothing can separate you from God even if you run away because His love will never fail you.

To the readers

My cordial regards to all the readers. I have written this book with prayer in my heart and belief that the readers will be blessed. During times of despair, sadness and sorrow despite knowing that God will answer our prayers in the right time we lose our faith in Him. The stories convey a very strong message that we should not give up even after repeated failures because God knows what's best for us.

The stories will give you the confidence to face failures and trials in your life. Some say that they are the only ones who are suffering in this world. Are you one of them? I have narrated the stories in brief and simple messages. Be humble and stay positive is perpetuity and keep yourself contented and happy. God bless you.

Contents

Preface 5
Message 6
To the readers 7
Chapter 1: Cast Forth **9**
The Life of Longshi 10
Chapter 2: Dark Horse **27**
The Life of Soren 28
Chapter 3: On the Rack **37**
The Worship Leader 38
Chapter 4: The Evening of Life **46**
Leang's Life 47
Chapter 5: To Pull One **57**
The Life of Anyem 58
Conclusion 67
Index 68

Chapter 1:

Cast Forth

Being a Christian does not mean you are content. Despite everything what we have been blessed with, we still complain. This story is about a man who had nothing good happen in his life since the day he was born and even after finding success it was just an infatuation. Love and acceptance were missing from his life so he started looking for them in the wrong places. 1 Timothy 6:10 says, "For the love of money is the root of all evil: which while some coveted after, they are erred from the faith and pierced themselves through with many sorrows."

The Life of Longshi

This is the story of a man who had lived a pathetic and deplorable life since childhood and who has not even known his parents his entire life. His life was repugnant and not consummate.

He was a man deprived of all the happiness when he was a child and had a nondescript life with lots of bad memories. He was petrified with the thought that he was of no avail in society. He was an independent man with enthusiastic and consummate good qualities when I first met him.

When I first met Longshi, he was wearing fine clothes and wore a nice pair of black shoes. His wrist watch was gold in color and his hair was nicely trimmed. He was tall and had a fair complexion. The way he presented himself was very admirable and respectful. He was a believer who found God as a beloved and loving father. He enjoyed the affection and care of God during every moment of his life especially during periods of trial and tribulation, pain and distress.

Longshi lived an ordinary and simple life in a small town called Kohima town. I met this man when I went to attend a healing crusade in a small village. The healing crusade was hosted in a prayer house for three days. It was in the month of November during Christmas season. The crusade was hosted by a local church and a few hundred people arrived to attend the program.

The attendants were provided with food, water and separate rooms to rest. The attendants who came to attend the crusade were from different tribes of Nagaland. I was also an attendant in the crusade and that's how I met Longshi. I was just a teenager when I first met him. After talking to him I felt that his testimony should be told and testified.

Meeting this young man was a blessing for me and that's why I want to share the blessing. He was in his late 30's when I met him for the first time. His story is similar to any poor family in society but what makes his story special is based on how he handled the situations since childhood. Usually we have good memories of our childhood but for this man it was very different. God had always been there with him and helped him stand on his feet despite all the obstacles in life he had to endure and face.

After the evening church service was over, I went straight to my room for a nap. I was listening to music and later rested for an hour. I woke up with a heavy headache and so I needed some fresh air. I was taking a stroll around in the prayer house compound for a while. There was a man sitting on the bench. I wanted to rest for a while and so I asked the man if I could take the empty space to sit. That is how Longshi and I met and started our conversation.

The conversation we had was interesting because we both had interest in music. He likes listening to rock music and slow songs. He had interest in sports as well. We were talking about how many celebrities sold their souls to the devil for fame and power. It was a good conversation we had. Out of the blue he asked me why I came to attend the crusade. I simply replied that I needed prayer.

Ordinary Nagas With Exceptional Stories

As we were having a good conversation, I asked him the same question. He told me that he came to thank God for everything that has been happening in his life. I was humbled by his answer because most of us Christians only keep on asking from God every time we pray. We hardly thank God when we pray. Honestly, I wanted to know what was really happening in his life that he came to thank God. So, I politely asked him if he could tell me his testimony. Without any hesitation he started telling me his story.

As a child all he wanted was a good bed to rest, good clothes, video games, toys and an education in a good school. But all of these privileges were foreign to him. He grew up without the love of his biological parents. He was born and abandoned at a public hospital because his mom died right after his birth.

The father was unknown and there was no one who came to claim him. So he was kept in the orphanage home to be taken care of. When he told me that he didn't even try to look for his biological father after he became a grown man, it was hard for me to believe. As he continued speaking, I asked him if he is comfortable telling me his story. In a very polite manner he said that he is just sharing his testimony and he is happy to tell.

The orphanage was situated in a remote area far from town. There were around fifty children in the orphanage and it was taken care by a very well to do business man named Tali. The orphanage had a big play ground and the environment was good for the children.

There were questions in Longshi's mind as to who his parents were. Every Father's day and Mother's day he wondered if his parents were alive. He is among the few people in the world who have never celebrated such special days. Often he would just stand outside the main gate for a long time thinking who will love him as their own child. He wanted someone to calm him when he cried and always was praying that he be adopted soon.

He would think for hours and hours that God has punished him by making him an orphan. But he tried to stop because he knew that these thoughts were making him sick. He thought that it's fair for some children to have so much in life, and other unfortunates like him who had nothing at all.

One fine Monday morning, a couple came to visit the orphanage and to adopt Longshi as their own son. He was eight years old. The husband was named Khamba and the wife was named as Emiro. Longshi was so excited thinking that he finally will have a comfortable life and will be loved by his new parents. But it was the complete opposite of what he thought. Khamba was a doctor in a private hospital and he was respected man in the society.

But the couple that adopted him had no respect for the marriage. Husband and wife are equal before God and have equal rights and responsibilities to make their family a heaven of happiness but it was the opposite. They did not render heart support to each other during distress, disaster and discomfort. Instead they were not happy with each other.

The couple that adopted him was very rude to him from the first day. The family was not a godly family and most of the days the father comes home drunk. Often they would quarrel over minor issues which flare up leading to violence. Longshi's stepdad would beat up his wife and force her to have sex with him. And it was disturbing because Longshi would always hear it all the time because he was in the next room.

The marriage was not over but the love of husband and wife was completely destroyed. Marital love is a great gift of God. Their marriage was not active, constant, and equally strong during all seasons of life. The relationship they had was meaningless because there was no love for each other. And the anger and frustrations was upon Longshi most of the time.

The couple was not happy because the husband blamed his wife for not bearing children. Outwardly, the family behaved well and civilized but like many families in society, but there was no peace at home. He was not allowed to address the couple as mom and dad. Instead he addressed them as uncle and aunty.

His neighbors would bully him on the way to school every single day. They would lay in wait for him to pass by. Longshi was always terrified of this because he was beaten up sometimes when bullied. And when he reported this to his stepdad, he won't even bother to say anything.

He was not treated as a son but most likely as a servant for the household chores. He slept on the floor and he ate left over food most days. Every day he would wait for the family to eat first and only after that he will eat. Life was not a bed of roses for him. He wore torn and old clothes because he didn't have much. His school uniforms were old and his school bag was very old as well. His shoes were torn and worn out. He had to wake up at five o' clock in the morning every day.

His lifestyle was very pathetic since childhood. The hardest hurdle for him to face as a child was the mockery from his own friends calling him a servant even in the school. Imagine if you are in his shoes, how will you feel when your own classmates or friends call you a servant? Longshi was made fun of most of the time in school.

The teachers didn't like him very much because his performance in academics was very poor. There was no one to appreciate him whenever he got good grades or passed an exam. It was a big deal for him because he was not good in his studies and he hardly got good grades.

The treatment he got from home was somehow bearable but being treated badly in school was very hard for him to bear. He always had the feeling that all his classmates were embarrassed to even talk to him. He wanted to have good friends but none of his classmates wanted to be his friend.

At school, he always sat at the last bench corner because no one wanted to sit near him. After returning from school, he had to rush to his room, get his clothes changed and start working again. He had to clean the house, wash dishes and cook. As Longshi was sharing his story, I was fascinated with the fact that he was telling me his story as though we were best friends.

But despite what was happening in school and at home, he at least got some peace of mind going to Sunday school on Sundays. The Sunday school teacher, Ajung, was nice to him and would give him extra sweets every Sunday. She was a very well behaved young and beautiful lady. She was short and had a blond hair.

Ajung was a godly woman and was happily married to a church deacon. Ajung was a woman of faith and treated all the children in Sunday school equally. Longshi felt very blessed because he was getting lots of attention and love from the Sunday school teacher. After he was adopted from the orphanage, his Sunday school teacher was the first person who loved him as her own son.

Knowing the condition of Longshi, she always treated him well. Longshi always felt good singing in Sunday school and he liked the attention he got from the other children. No children in the Sunday school made fun of him and this made him happy and not ignored. The Sunday school teacher would always remind the children that God is the omnipresent, omnipotent and omniscient. He is our creator, sustainer and guardian and provider and protector. He memorized that line and wrote it down in the notebook as well.

Longshi told me that he was a loner and didn't have a best friend during his childhood days. It was really hard for me to believe that. He was bad in sports and weak in the field of academics as well. He had no talents whatsoever as a kid. But his goodness was in being gentle and humble. He learned how to pray at Sunday school. He would recite the Sermon on the Mount before prayer.

As he was narrating the story to me, he suddenly stopped and starting laughing. I wondered what could have possibly made him laugh. He told me that once he went to attend a birthday party without the knowledge of his step parents. He wore clean clothes and his school shoes to attend the birthday party. The birthday boy was his classmate and he thought of going because all of his classmates were making plans to attend the party.

It was on the Saturday morning he bought a birthday card. When he reached the gate he was a bit relieved because he saw many of his classmates playing around outside the compound and having a good time. He could see through the window that there were lots of people inside.

He felt a bit reluctant to enter the room because he was having second thoughts. It so happened that when he knocked on the door, the birthday boy came running and opened the door with such excitement expecting more gifts. But when the birthday boy opened the door, there were no signs of any happiness.

Instead, Longshi was asked why he came. At that moment Lonsghi was speechless. The birthday boy told him that he is not invited. Without saying a word, Lonsghi went back home. That day he was troubled with the thoughts of rejection and humiliation from his classmates.

Longshi was gifted a small Bible from the Sunday school class. He loved reading it whenever he got time. At times, he would think that maybe living in the orphanage would have been better because at least he had some friends and he didn't have to work so much when he was living in the orphanage.

Till the age of sixteen years, he suffered and went through a lot of pain and stress. He always had faith in God that he will find success in the future. Life was not treating him well. Longshi wanted so many things in life but it was of no avail because all he could do was pray and wait for God to do miracles.

He started to smile and he stopped talking. I was curious as to why he was not continuing with the story. After two minutes, he told me that he fell in love with a girl but it was of no avail because that girl didn't even reply when he tried talking to her. The name of the girl was Shomla and she was two years younger than him and they studied in the same school he was enrolled in.

Shomla was a pianist and she was a stage performer as well. During school functions, she would play musical recitals and musical pieces. Longshi's admired her very much since their school days but he was helpless. It was really funny when Longshi told me that he would clap and cheer so loudly after Shomla's performance on stage.

Longshi wanted to be friends with her so desperately but he felt that he really is a servant and need not to mingle with anyone.

Growing up was no joke for him but he had faith in God that he will find true happiness and freedom soon. When Longshi was in his tenth standard, the couple who adopted him divorced due to domestic violence at home and misbehavior from the husband. The separation was not a shock for him because he knew that sooner or later this would happen.

Neither of them wanted to keep Longshi with them. This was again another big issue for him because the constant thought that he is really useless and unwanted kept bothering him. He had nowhere to go. But as per the contract made by the couple during the adoption, the husband had to pay for Longshi's needs till he finishes his studies.

He was shifted to a boy's hostel and he was given monthly allowance to pay his college fees and tuition fees. The hostel he was admitted in was old and the surroundings were not hygienic. It was an old building with lots of repairing and coloring needed.

His stepfather admitted him in an Arts college in Kohima town. The college was not as bad as he described. There were thousands of students enrolled in that college. There was a basketball court, badminton court and a small stadium for playing indoor games.

Again, Longshi was left alone without a family. Longshi told me that he didn't get any negative approach and humiliation from the hostel and college. It was really hard for him to accept the fact that life was treating him really bad. He was devastated because all he wanted was a family and a good life. The one thing that kept him happy was when he read the Bible and prayed. That was the only comfort he got.

Like any teenager, he had lots of wants and needs but sadly he hardly had any money. After paying the hostel mess fees and college fees, he hardly had any money left to end the month. But somehow, he managed to use the money wisely.

He was suffering the sadness of an orphan in difficult times and situations. Sometimes he found it hard to bear the bitterness of solitude and agony.

He started making new friends and getting involved in social functions and organizations. He joined as a member in the Red Ribbon Club and Eco Club. He became an active member. Longshi had no talent in him but his good natured behavior and humble attitude made him approachable and he was able to make many new friends. Longshi was happy because things were taking a different turn in his life.

One Friday morning, he saw an advertisement in the newspaper. It read as, part time job vacancy in a general store. The store was six kilometers r from the hostel he was staying at. He was interested and so he applied for the job. After a month, he got the job and his work was to sell gadgets and books.

After college hours, he would find customers and sell the products. Most days, he would request his roommate to keep his evening share of food in the container. He was working very hard to earn his pocket money and he slept for only five hours in a day because he had to sleep late and wake up very early.

He always returned to the hostel late at night despite repeated warning from the warden. And finally one night, he was kicked out of the hostel because he came in at midnight. The warden got very angry and he chased him out of the hostel. It was raining very heavily and there were neither bus services nor any cabs. He had nowhere to go and so he had to spend the night in someone's rice field.

The next morning, he went back to hostel and begged the warden to understand his situation. But the warden didn't listen and told him that he can't reinstate him in the hostel. Longshi tried to control his emotions and he left by saying thanks to the warden.

With the little savings he had, he moved to a cheap rental. The house had no windows and there was no electricity in the room. He had to use candles and a kerosene lamp at night. The room was very dirty and was not painted. But he had to take the place because the rent was cheap and reasonable. He had to continue his part time work as a salesman because he needed pocket money.

Somehow, he was managing to support himself but again another huge wave was coming in his life. He was dropped out of college due to his low attendance. He wrote and appeal to the principal of the college but it was not granted. His appeal was rejected because he was warned many times about his poor attendance.

This was a huge turning point for Longshi because he knew that his stepfather will not take responsibility anymore in helping him financially. Since he had to support himself, he had no choice but to take a break in his education. Now he was on his own and there was no one to help him financially.

He worked very hard as a sales man and always managed to reach the targets set by his boss every month. His boss was so happy with his hard working attitude and service. Gradually, he was promoted as an accountant in the general store he was working for. He worked there for a few years and managed to save sufficient money. But he was not satisfied working as an accountant.

He decided to leave the job because he didn't want to spend the rest of his life working for someone else. So he left the job and decided to start his own business. With the experience he had, he was determined to work hard and find success. Finally, he decided to be a dealer in gadgets and musical instruments.

He managed to make partnership with a businessman. His business expanded very swiftly and he would earn more than he needed every month. There were rapid sales and the promotion of his business was very good. His business was flourishing because he already had the skill of speaking and getting customers interested in the goods.

He managed to buy a new car with insurance. And he also bought a land with a house in town area. The new house he bought was located in a peaceful environment. He took a bank loan and established his own shops that dealt with buying and selling of gadgets. Now he was happy and content since he became the boss of his own business and stores.

As he was getting used to a comfortable lifestyle and earning more money, he was forgetting that it was God helping him. He would skip morning and evening prayers and stopped going to church as well. He stopped giving ten tithes to the church. He was drawn more towards what human flesh desires. He was chasing after sexual fantasies to fill the emptiness inside him. His bondage was towards drugs and alcohol.

He became very good friends with one of his business partner. His business partner was an atheist and he would always say that the existence of God is not true. He always spoke against the canons and the Ten Commandments in the Holy Scripture. Sometimes Longshi would start questioning himself if there is really a God. That's when the devil began working in his mind. It's true that sometimes bad company of friends will mislead you. His friend would make fun of Christians. He quoted that the husband and wife that have been fighting the whole day comes to the church with a big smile on their face, sit next to each other and pretend that nothing happened.

Life took a different turn for Longshi as he was fulfilling his dreams of having a comfortable lifestyle. He got everything he wanted and he never looked back. He started to indulge himself in alcohol, drugs and immoral activities. He traveled abroad to further his business career and was even more confident in what he was capable of.

He became popular among his locality and friends as well unlike when he was a child. Having forgotten the fact that it was God who have given him everything he wanted, and made him a successful man. He was blindsided by his success and fame he got from his business. But he didn't know that he was living a life of infatuation.

One fine Wednesday afternoon when Longshi went for shopping, he met his old Sunday school teacher Ajung. He hugged her and said thank you. Ajung could not recognize him. Longshi introduced himself and reminded her that he was her student. Ajung smiled and told him that she will always keep him in her prayers. Longshi asked her if she wanted anything. Ajung simply replied that all she wants from him is that he be happy and successful in life.

Life was rolling smoothly for him but in between the years 2007 – 2009, he had a downfall in his business. The ties with his business friends were feeble because of his poor performance and low capital. His business partners lost faith in him because he was not taking his job seriously. Failure in his business was very new to him.

One of his stores caught fire and it destroyed many imported goods and valuable antiques in the shop. The insurance didn't pay off completely as well. There were fewer customers and the goods he sold were not reaching the expectations of the buyers. His well established shops were shut down and he hit rock bottom. He was broke and had huge payment due to the bank.

The past repeated itself again. His friends refused to help him and ignored his calls. Longshi had problems with sexual desires and alcohol. It became worse when he faced failure on a daily basis. He had to sell the house and most of his assets were taken by the bank because Longshi was unable to pay on time.

He took shelter in a house that he rented for few months. It was a small room with no toilet attached and no water supply. Longshi had nothing left with him except some clothes and a few books. His life was so pathetic that he even had to sell his watch and shoes for food and water.

One evening, he decided to sell his old books to pay his rent. While arranging the books, there was one magazine that caught his eye. As he started flipping over the pages, he found this Bible verse, "Have patience, God isn't finished yet", from the book of Philippians 1:6. He sat down and continued reading for hours.

Later that night, he had a sleepless night. He thought of everything that had happened to him since his childhood days and how God helped him become a successful man. He wept bitterly thinking how he turned away from God. The big question he asked himself was why God still loved him so much.

The next day, he prayed and made up his mind to live a good life. He left all the bad habits and tried to turn away from the foolish ways. The first thing he did was forgive his friends for not helping him in times of need. He wanted to meet his step parents but both of them refused to meet him. So he sent them a letter each telling them which read, "I forgive you for not treating me like a son and I thank you for everything you had done for me." It was not easy to write this because Lonsghi still remembered how he was treated when he was a child.

Months passed by and he was trying hard to convince his old business partners to help him. He knew it was never too late for him. It was really hard for him to face the same problems he faced as a child. He tried a different outlook in life and did not relinquish his hopes in moving forward despite the obstacles.

He worked day and night as a small retailer and saved enough money to start a business. Gradually, he managed to start saving money and could afford a good place to rent. Today, he is contended with what he has. Longshi told me that he is not as rich as he was before but he was happy and contented with his life. This is what he quoted, "God accepted me despite of who I am."

After he told me his testimony, I was blessed and glad that I met such a wonderful person. I wished him good night and went to my room. After listening to his story, I was wondering how life treats people in a different way. Behind every smile there is really a painful story. Attending the crusade was a blessing for me. And the next day I wanted to talk to him again but I couldn't find him.

We are often worried and set back with our thoughts. Failure scares us and gives us the negative aspect to give up. Most of us keep comparing ourselves with others and that's why we are never contented.

There are millions of unhappy people today. It's because we only dream and dream. Hard work and determination will never fail you. Longshi didn't give up despite the repeated failures, mockery and rejections in life. It's very true that failure means giving up without trying again and again.

Don't let you failures define you. Believing in yourself is your greatest weapon to any and every obstacle in life. Living a life of compunction is meaningless. Instead of that you can be contented with what God has given you and live a life of celibacy.

If Longshi hadn't believed in himself then what would he be now? There are people who don't accept themselves as strong individuals. They are comfortable living under the shadows of someone else. God has his own ways and plans to reach us. No matter how many plans we make and strive for, only God knows what the future will be.

The book of Romans 8:18 read, "For I reckon that the sufferings of this present time are not worthy to be compared with the glory which shall be revealed in us." The Bible speaks of Paul, Peter and John's confidence in suffering. Longshi was in depression after the downfall of his business and that's when he started to look for happiness in the wrong places. This is the problem many of us face; we pursue happiness but often in the wrong places. Find refuge in Jesus and he will lead your path.

Longshi had a spiritual depression which was caused by sin. He let money exercise power over him and it blinded him to the power money has. He let his guard down and that's when the devil took advantage of his weakness. Sometimes God permits temptation to come upon us that we may know ourselves and feel our own weakness.

Chapter 2:

Dark Horse

People make wrong decisions when they are angry and not in their right mind. Many Christians don't understand the concept of patience and tolerance. When God don't answer their prayers on time they get restless and start questioning God. This particular story is about a man who blamed himself for the death of his father. His mother was a lady of faith who was always positive about all the temptations and trials the family was facing, hoping and praying that God will provide in the right time. The book of Proverbs 16:9 reads, "A man's heart deviseth his way but the Lord directeth his steps."

The Life of Soren

This young man I met was a godly man and comes from a Christian family. He seemed to be joyful and in a good mood most of the time. I paid a visit to my friend Thovi and that's how I met him. Thovi is a good friend of mine and we studied in the same college. Thovi introduced me to one of his best friends, Soren. Soren seemed like a good man and a person of interest. He was a short and handsome young man with dark colored hair.

After a week, I invited my friends for my birthday party. I was having a good time with my friends. Thovi told me that Soren has sent his regards for my birthday. I asked Thovi what Soren's story was. I was startled when my friend, Thovi, told me about Soren's story. His story can be conducive in nature for many people who have a frivolous concept on struggle and temptations.

Behind that bright smile of his, there was a very painful story. No one would have thought that this young man had such consolidated faith as a Christian. He was born and raised from a middle class family. They lived in a small house constructed from bamboo and timber.

Soren's family didn't live a luxurious life but they were happy. Soren's father was named Chumbemo and his mother's name as Beni. Soren had a sister named Kathi. Soren's mom was unemployed and his father was a laborer as a stone miner. Soren's father was a kind man and a man of a few words. Soren's family always had a time of prayer every evening. Life was not so hard for the family until one fateful day.

One fine morning, his father had lunch and went to work as usual. There was an accident in the stone mine where his father worked. Within a blink of an eye, there were hundreds of stones rolling towards him. He ran as fast as he could but to no avail. His legs were caught in the huge pile of rocks. There was lots of blood spilled on the floor. His fellow workers helped him remove the stones. He fainted and was breathing very heavily. He was rushed to a government hospital. Later that evening, the doctor gave the bad news to the family that his father was paralyzed from the waist down and cannot walk anymore. There were many well-wishers who came to visit his father and he was discharged when he started to recover.

The fact that his father was paralyzed was such a huge disappointment because his mom was unemployed at that moment as well and there was no one with a job to look after the family. Soren was just eight years old when this tragedy happened and his sister Kathi was still in high school. Being the only son in the family, Soren started to think that he should look after the family.

The compensation money and relief payment given to the father was already spent. The costs of medicines and weekly treatment for his father were too high. On top of that, the well-wishers would stop coming and helping them. At this stage, Soren's mom was helpless as she had to feed her children. She had used up all the savings in her husband's treatment.

The condition of the family was getting deplorable and there were very few helping hands. Soren's mom was a woman of faith and had a very cordial nature. Despite the huge problems, she always conducted evening prayer meetings every day with her family. The father was helpless because he couldn't do anything as he was still recovering from his leg injury.

His mom applied for many jobs but since she didn't have any educational qualifications it was hard to find a job. As the days were passing by, she became more desperate to find a job to feed the family. They were living in such a condition that having three square meals per day was a privilege. Soren's mom was a woman of faith and a true believer. The book of Luke 7:12-16 talks about the widow of Nain whose son was resurrected by Jesus. Soren's mother had full faith in God that her family would prosper.

There were days when they had to go to sleep without food and they couldn't afford good clothes. Soren's mom sold some of the good furniture they had and paid the school fees. She even had to sell the unused utensils she kept for special occasions. She was induced to sell the things because of the deplorable condition the family was in.

The situation was insidious and the family had to suffer even more. Soren's mom felt impotent and indigent without a job and without financial stability. She collected eatable mushrooms and leafs from the jungle and would sell vegetables as a vendor in the market and that's how she was trying to feed her children and pay for the medicines for her husband.

One day when she was collecting eatable leafs from the jungle, a snake bit her on her hand and she fainted there on the spot. She was helped by a local farmer who found her in the jungle. He quickly sucked and spitted the venom and brought her safe to her home. After two hours when she woke up, she found herself surrounded by her family and neighbors. That night she testified in the family prayer meeting that she didn't die because God is always watching over her.

Along with his sister, Soren started to collect wasted aluminum cans, slightly rusted irons and old utensils found in drains and rivers. And they sold it to the junk dealers for pocket money. I clearly remember him telling me that he had no option other than that.

There was a day when the junk dealer didn't come to their locality. The same happened the next four days. Finally after a week when the junk dealer came to their colony, he rushed towards him and called him with delight in his heart.

One day, his elder sister told him that she wanted to eat mangoes that were growing in the garden of their neighbor. After school was over, Soren quietly went to steal the mangoes but sadly he was caught by the proud owner of the mango tree. He punished Soren hitting him with a stick and he made him sweep the dry leafs in the entire garden.

After Soren came home crying, his mom asked him what happened. He told his mom the whole story. His mom got so angry that she went straight to the person who punished her son. Instead of being embarrassed, the neighbor started shouting at her. He was scolding her by telling her that her son is a thief and useless like his crippled father.

Soren's mom knew that even if she keeps on quarrelling it will be of no avail. So she just told him that she forgave him for punishing her kid. After returning back home, she punished

Soren and went straight to the kitchen. She locked herself in and started crying silently. She felt so depressed because she couldn't afford to buy fruits for her children.

It so happened that one time Soren didn't return home for a week. The first night his mom thought that he was having a sleep over at his friend's house. The next day he didn't return home. This created panic and fear in the minds of his family. The whole family was restless and started looking for him. Soren's family went to the police station seeking for help. Even the police couldn't find him. All of the neighbors were searching for him as well.

The colony youths formed many search parties and went looking for him. Days passed by and still there was no news about where he was. Soren's family was so helpless that they were having sleepless nights thinking what could have happened to him. Her mom fasted and prayed for days.

She had faith that God will keep Soren safe and secure. The church members and the pastor also visited his family and prayed for him. As the days were passing by, the people started to lose hope that he was alive. But Soren's mom didn't lose hope on her son's life. After a week, he came back home smiling with lots of contentment in his heart.

Without saying a word, his mom started hitting him with a bamboo stick. She didn't listen to what Soren was trying to say. After a few minutes, he reached into his pocket and took out a two hundred rupees note, gave it to mom and said he worked very hard to earn the money.

His mom got even angrier and started beating him some more. Soren cried and replied, "You can hit me more Mom but please keep the money, because we need it." Soren told his mom that he worked on a small farm to earn the money. He was feeding the pigs and was looking after the cows. He worked the whole day and the farmer gave him cow's milk and rice for lunch and dinner every day.

Soren told his mother that he was treated well and he had really worked very hard for the money. He slept inside the farm house and he was given a blanket by the owner of the farm. Hearing this, Soren's mom wept bitterly and told him never to repeat this again. She told him that God has helped us survive and He will never leave us. God knows what's best for us and will give us what we need in the right time.

This was a very pathetic moment for Soren's dad as well. He thought he was the reason why his son had to do this. His father was crying out loud and was blaming himself. After the accident, Soren's father had been a huge burden to his own family.

There was lots of money being spent on his medicines and treatment expenditures. His dad thought that ending his life would lessen the family problems. At times like this, the devil always takes advantage of the situation. His dad might have thought of many negative thoughts that really touched his heart and disturbed his mind.

Soren's dad called him and talked with him for few minutes. I don't know what conversation they had. But I am sure his father knew that it would be their last conversation. Soren had no idea what was going on in his dad's mind. His father let fear become a burden to his family. Soren's father told him to shut the door as he left the room. Later that evening, Soren's father reached for a razor blade on the table and ended his life with a silent death. He could not overcome the fear of death and dying by looking forward to heaven.

After two hours when Soren's mom entered the room, she found her husband dead. She called out to her children and all the neighbors came rushing after hearing the loud screaming and weeping. The room was occupied with many people. The church members came and the colony prayer group also came to comfort the family. The funeral service was held the next day and his dad was buried in a common public cemetery.

After the burial of his dead father, Soren felt responsible for his father's death. He started hearing voices in his head. He was going insane because he kept telling himself that he is the reason for his dad's death.

At one point of time, I asked my friend, Thovi, how he knows so much about his friend Soren. He replied that he can't forget every detail about Soren's story. After the incident, Thovi would spend many hours with Soren trying to comfort him. This was why Thovi knew so much about his friend's story.

Soren's mom and sister tried comforting him telling him it's not his fault but he didn't listen. He kept on blaming himself. Weeks passed by and he was trying to keep himself occupied. Things were getting better eventually for him and his family.

After a year, his mom got a sweeper's job in a government office. Gradually there was crescendo in financial income as well. After completing high school, his sister managed to get a job in an office.

Soren decided to study theology after finishing higher secondary. He stopped regretting of what happened in his life because it cannot be changed, undone or forgotten. He tried to move on with his life and he got sponsorship from the church to pursue studying theology. I don't know what could have been the reason for him to pursue theology.

Despite all the short comings and trials his family had to face, they never lost faith in God. Faith without work is dead because your enemy doesn't spare anything. At one point of time, the situation for the family became so horrid and deplorable that Soren's mom thought of giving her children up for adoption as she didn't have any financial source of income. But she managed to hitch and balance the situation though prayer and fasting.

Soren's mom had patience and tolerance in her life and she never questioned God about the situation she was in. She was waiting for God to work miracles in his own time. It's a lesson for many because there are people who would complain as to why God is not helping despite of what he or she is doing for the glorification of the Lord. The Bible teaches us that if God is with us then nobody can stand against us.

We always expect something back after every good deed we do. But as a Christian, we never realize that God is almighty and is watching our every move that we make. We as humans have the tendency to forget and do what pleases us the most. This world is not our home and we are just a traveler. Make your life on earth blessed and meaningful.

Soren's dad took his own life thinking he was a burden to his family. He could have overcome the fear of death by remembering that he had a purpose in life. If a person takes his or her own life, they will never go to heaven. If only Soren's father would have had patience to overcome his fears of giving up. The Bible reads that one should be reconciled with God to overcome the fear of death or dying.

Chapter 3:
On the Rack

"And when thou prayest, thou shalt not be as the hypocrites are: for they love to pray standing in the synagogues and in the corners of the streets, that they may be seen. Verily I say unto you, they have their reward." I felt the need to quote this from the bible because the story of Meang is connected to the verse. This is the story of a man who lived a double life. His story is a lesson for many of us Christians. We may be involved in ministries and many good charity groups but God is always watching our every move. We cannot escape his punishment. This is the story of a man who was punished by God.

The Worship Leader

My grandma, Lomi Omie, told me many stories whenever she felt like it. She would always cook for me and she would teach me songs and read to me many a times. One fine Sunday morning, my grandma told me a very interesting story about a man named Meang, a man with great talents in music and arts and he had a very good sense of humor. As a young teenager, he also had a very short tempered nature but his testimony is worth telling.

Meang was a very busy man actively involved in doing missionary works and he was a musician as well. He would visit many places and pray for the sick in hospitals, rehab centers and remote places with no electricity and water supply. He was an executive member in the local church as well and was a very fine young gentleman actively working for the Lord. The society respected him and would encourage him in keeping up with the good work.

Meang grew up in a well to do family as a child. His childhood was good because he got everything he wanted and needed. He was educated from a good private school and a reputed college as well. Meang didn't have any regrets in life because everything was going on just fine in his life. His parents were also well qualified and educated. Meang was the only child in the family. That's also the reason he got so much attention and love from his parents.

He had everything he wanted and was contented with his life. He was a very smart and educated teenager before he committed the crime. He could sing and play different types of instruments and he was good in paintings and art as well. He composed his own songs and would perform in many stages and public gatherings. With such good art skills and music talents he was living a good and respected life. He had good company of friends and he was very sociable person as well.

One fine day, Meang and his friends went out for a picnic in the jungle for hiking and rock climbing. It was a peaceful day and the weather was very pleasant. They left for the picnic early in the morning. He was having a good time with his friends. They drove for an hour and finally reached their destination. They had packed eatables, drinking water and all the necessary tools for fishing and ropes.

They cooked good food, went fishing, rock climbing, etc. It was around four o'clock in the evening when he and his friends were taking rest around a bond fire. They were singing, talking and having good moments.

As they were talking, all out of sudden there was a huge misunderstanding among the friends. The exchange of words became abusive and led to physical violence. Meang, who was in his 30s, got so angry at his friend, Peter, that he accidently hit him with a slab of wood. Within few minutes, his friend fell down on the ground and was drop dead. The murder was not intentional.

Meang didn't know how to react after what he did. None of them had a telephone. He was apologizing to his friend, Peter, again and again but it was of no avail. His other friends were also not sure what to do. The situation was too tense.

Meang was arrested and was on trial for murder. He was however allowed to pay his last respect for few minutes at the funeral. At the funeral, the mother of Peter came straight forward at him and slapped him on his face. She didn't say anything and turned her face around. People were judging him with such hatred in their eyes and gave him a very negative look. The people who once praised him and admired him were the ones who were judging him.

When he was in jail, he was having a very hard time trying to adjust. Meang was living a life of pain and regret inside the jail. In the first few weeks, all he did was weep and cry day and night. He was kept on duty to clean the toilets and the compound of the jail every day. If he skipped even a day, he was punished.

He thought that his life is over and there was nothing left in his life. Because of the felony he committed, his family was put to disgrace and shame. There were thousands of voices he could hear in his head telling him that his life is over.

There was no sign of happiness and joy in his life. He questioned God as to why his friend had to die with just one hit. He got even angrier and pissed at God. There was no reason for him to get mad at God. This is the reality of many of the Christians. We keep on complaining and fail to appreciate what God has done for us so. We always keep on expecting more from God.

Meang was suffering in the jail and his family members would come to visit him in the jail once in a week. There was nothing that could give him peace of mind. Meang's parents hired a very good lawyer for the trial but it was to no avail. Inside the jail, nobody knew him unlike when he was in the society. At one point of time, he was kept in the solitary confinement for beating another prisoner black and blue.

The reason for this act was because the injured prisoner teased him for killing his friend with his own hand. Meang was already in somber and he lost his temper again. At first, he didn't want to hit him but the injured prisoner was talking more nonsense with abusive and offensive words to him.

Every Sunday there was a worship service conducted by the Chaplin inside the jail compound. It was not mandatory for the prisoners to attend the fellowship services. One day, the Chaplin called for Meang in his office. He read a bible verse from the book of Proverbs 28:13 which says, "He that covereth his sin shall not prosper: but whoso confesseth and forsaketh them shall have mercy." They had a time of prayer and counseling. The Chaplin gifted a Bible to him and requested him to attend the fellowship on Sundays.

The Chaplin's first counseling had no effect on Meang because he was still somber. Meang was still very upset and refused to mingle with his cellmates and other prisoners. Prayer and fellowships were nothing more than just a time for gathering. He completely lost faith in God and he was always trying to confine himself in the cell. He won't even eat some days.

Meang's life was sad and very pathetic. One particular night, he had a very bad dream. He woke up around two o'clock in the morning crying and sweat was all over his body. His cellmates were also awakened by his loud crying and shouting. They gave him water to drink and tried talking to him. The next morning, he requested the jail guards to tell the Chaplin that he wanted to meet him. After few days, the Chaplin came to meet with Meang.

Meang narrated the dream to the Chaplin and told him that he can't live with the guilt of murder anymore. Meang started speaking what was in his heart and he told the Chaplin everything that was bothering him. He explained the thoughts that keep disturbing his mind and the voices he was hearing telling him that his life is over. The Chaplin prayed for him and told him that everything will be alright.

Meang would read the Bible every day and ponder on it and he started attending the fellowship on Sundays. He started to take interest in music again and he soon became the Praise and Worship Leader in the fellowship conducted every Sunday inside the jail campus.

The man who had been confined in his cell most of the time, started preaching and singing among his other fellow prisoners. Some of the prisoners who never attended the church also started to attend fellowships with the inspiration they got from Meang. This was the sign that was showing how God was using His humble child, Meang, inside the jail

Meang finally found a reason to live and was contented again. He was in prison for a long time but he was still different from before. His way of presenting himself was different and he was always reading good Christian books during his free time. He realized that he acted in a false manner and was insincere and hypocritical pretending to obey and serve God.

Meang's testimony was a blessing to many. In his dream, he dreamt about all the erroneous ways he was in. There were flashbacks of the things he did and who he used to be. Everything was so real in his dream and he saw everything in crystal clear images.

Meang was involved in a Christian ministry when he was a teenager. But secretly he was a chain smoker and he was an alcoholic as well. These were some of the darkest secrets he had that no one knew about him.

Meang confessed that he has been punished by God because he was not leading a good life. He was involved in church works and was a very active member in the church but he was not living a practical life. Meang worked as a missionary but he knowingly kept on making lots of mistakes. He didn't live a life of a true Christian and that's the reason God punished him.

I felt the need to share this story because sometimes it's never what you think it is. You may be involved in many ministries, voluntary works and many good deeds. But sometimes all God wants is a clean and a faithful heart. What if Meang didn't get a chance to change his double life and die?

God gave another chance to the city of Nineve to change their ways of living through Jonah. Every one of us gets another chance to change our lives again and again but we just ignore God's warnings. Sometimes we become so judgmental and that's when the devil takes advantage of our thoughts.

Jonah went up the hill and was waiting for God to destroy Nineveh. He got angry when God didn't destroy the city as he said he would. God told Jonah that he gave another chance to Nineve like he gave him another chance. Sometimes we take pleasure in someone else's misery.

Ordinary Nagas With Exceptional Stories

Many people do not practice what they preach. Meang was actively involved in working for the Lord but he was living a double life. Meang was living a life of a Christian who was actively working for God's glory and at the same time living a different life outside the church. Vain and useless discourses are a great burden to the spiritual growth and especially to a weary spiritual mind that needs betterment.

He was a person who would leave his sins at the door before he entered the church. No one knew that he was not living an honest life. He was pretending to be a faithful Christian who was tirelessly working for the Lord. But deep down, Meang knew that he was not living a practical life. He was different when he was in the church and had a different life outside church. This is the reality for many of us Christians.

Not just this but many youth have been drawn towards lust and enjoyment. When there is no one around, young people have the tendency to surf the net for pornographic images, dirty magazines and uncensored sites. The habit of speaking lies and bearing false witness against their neighbors are also sins. Some become professional liars that they don't feel any regret in telling a lie to anyone, not even their family. A Christian will realize when he has committed sin and he tries not to repeat it again. But there are some Christians who keep on involving themselves in bad habits that they get too comfortable with sin. And it no longer bothers them that they are committing sin.

My conscious is clear in telling this story because I want to obstruct all those people involved in doing well by conveying a message that God will judge you and not your works you have done for him. Jonah disobeyed God and he tried to hide from him.

But there is nothing we can hide from God. Teachers may teach the doctrine, true and useful but without putting it to action it is dead. That's when Satan may abuse and pervert scripture. Try to keep calm and be still, humbling yourself under the mighty hand of God.

Chapter 4:
The Evening of Life

The book of Proverbs 15:3 says "The eye of the Lord is everywhere. No one can run away and hide from God." This story is about a strong lady who led a life of pain and sorrow. Her story is so inspiring because she was a true Christian with a positive outlook in life no matter how many times she was forced to give up. She continued to thank God in all the circumstances for this is the will of God.

Leang's Life

I haven't met her personally but her story is worth knowing. This story is about a mother who scarified everything for her children. I was fascinated when I first heard her story. I went to attend a festival in my hometown, Nagaland, a state in India known as a land of festivals. There are many festivals celebrated for different tribes every year in the state.

When I reached the venue, there were thousands of people. All of them dressed in their own colorful attires and ornaments. They were all in a festive mood and the set up for the festival was so good. Food was served using banana leaves and water was served using cups made of bamboos. The elders gave speeches and there were dance performances and lots of presentations. Out of the four speakers, I was really inspired by the message a lady named Miss Aria shared with the people. She talked about life's struggle and victory in hard work.

I was sitting next to an elderly man dressed up in his traditional attire. He wore a big cone shaped cap with a hornbill feather at the edge of his cap, earrings, tight short pants and his body was tattooed. He didn't wear a shirt and had a machete and long spear with him. After the lady's speech was over, I asked the person sitting next to me about her. He told me that the speaker is the daughter of Leang.

After the festival program was over, I drove back home. I asked my uncle who Leang was. My uncle started to laugh out loud and asked me why I wanted to know. To be honest, I really don't know why I asked.

My uncle told me that Leang was a very powerful motivational speaker in the tribe. She was respected by the people for who she was. I was interested in knowing more about her. When I asked him what she looked like, my uncle told me that all he could remember was that she had curly hair. I wondered what made her such a renowned person among the tribe.

Then my uncle started narrating Leang's story to me. Leang was married to a policeman when she was in her mid 20's. It was an arranged marriage and the reception was in the church. My uncle didn't describe about Leang's husband much Except that he was an educated and respected man.

Her family was free from poverty and financial problems. God blessed her with two children named Zakho and Aria. Life was static and comfortable for the family and Leang was very contented. However, she never knew that her life was going to change completely. It was in the month of January that she celebrated her wedding anniversary with her husband. They hosted a big party that day and had many invitees. I asked my uncle how he remembered even the month of her anniversary. He told me that he knows because he would attend the seminars and programs where Leang spoke. So that's how he knows the details about her story.

Little did she know that life was going to be so harsh to her. The next day after the wedding anniversary celebration, her husband died when she was pregnant with third child. She had been waiting for the right time to give the news to her husband about her being pregnant with the third child. She started slapping his face and was crying out loud calling his name telling him to wake up but there was complete silence in the room.

Her life changed completely after her husband's death. There were many people who came to pay their last respect on the funeral day. After the burial of her late husband, she returned home with her children wishing this was just a bad dream. That day, she locked herself in the bedroom and she did not speak to anyone. She was still in shock and cried the whole night. But she had to be strong for her kids. She knew that crying won't do her any good. Everything was going wrong in her life and all hope seemed to fade away. She was lonely and depressed but she didn't allow the enemy to convince her that she was alone because God was with her.

After two months, she had used up all of the money she had saved and there was just a few assets left with her. She became broke and had no money left to support her family. She applied for her late husband's pension but it was taking a lot of time. Her condition was so pathetic and deplorable. She had to sell her husband's assets the family car, which was an old Jeep. She even had to sell the house and move to a small apartment with no running water and poor furniture. The four sides of the walls were old and the construction was very feeble. And there were no well-wishers to welcome them to the neighbourhood. Moving to a new house was hard for her family and she found it very hard to adjust to the new lifestyle.

She would come across many people who were once good friends with her husband but they all just passed by without even talking to her. None of the friends of her late husband helped her in these times of need. Leang felt impotent and helpless with such treatment she was getting from her neighbors and people she was once friends with. Her neighbors were not good to them and some nights people would throw stones on the roof of the house. After a few months, the owner of the house forced her to move out because she didn't pay the rent for four months.

Before her husband's death, Leang had many friends. However, Leang was happy because at least she had one good friend Ekali, who was good to Leang's children, treated her well and with respect. Ekali helped Leang find a cheaper house to rent.

She was finding it hard to live such a pathetic life. But she had to face the reality and give up so many things for the family. Out of all the assets she sold, the most valuable instrument was the grand piano. That was the sweetest memory she had of her late husband. He would play the piano for her on every special occasion. That same piano was used at her wedding.

Despite all the issues and hardships she was facing, Leang refused to accept defeat and was determined that she will not let herself down. She never missed a day without prayer and meditation. Every day she would wake up around four o'clock and pray for her family. She never let kindness and truth leave her and she believed that God has a better plan for her family. Although they were poor and needy, she somehow managed to pay the school fees of her children.

Leang parents were farmers and they couldn't help her much financially. Her parents lived in the village and hardly visited her. News spread like wild fire in the village about how she was struggling and finding it hard to manage the family needs.

The villagers were not happy about it and thought of helping her. It was good because the villagers decided to help her but not every helping hand is worth accepting. One night, all the village elders came to visit her and they made the wrong decision and proposed to adopt and raise her kids. She denied because she didn't like the idea of staying away from her children. She refused and said that she rather die than to be separated from her children.

When she opposed to the idea of adoption, an elder stood up and scolded her. He quoted that she was making a mistake because she was still not mature enough. One by one, the elders started to advice her. But she kept quiet for a while. And finally she stood up from her seat and told the elders that she will never be separated from her kids as long as she lives. She added that she doesn't mean to disrespect the village, but she won't mind even if she is not allowed to enter the village because her children are more important.

This was such a disappointment for her because she couldn't accept the fact that the villagers even thought of such thing. They proposed that her two children would be adopted by two different relatives and her children would be fed well but they would have to work in the rice field and help in doing household works. This was just a prudent way of saying that her children would work as a helper.

Leang's parents were angry at her because she didn't accept the proposal. They were terrified as to how she would manage to look after her children. Leang did not blame her parents for suggesting that because she knew that her parents didn't want her to suffer so much. And on top of that, she was pregnant without a job. Leang was determined to work hard and she didn't give up yet. One insult that she found very hard to accept was when her neighbors would spit at the gate of her house while passing by. This was too much for her to handle but she forgave them and prayed for them instead.

On one occasion, there was celebration for parent's day. She borrowed a dress from her friend, Ekali, to wear. She didn't have any good clothes to wear because she sold all her good clothes along with the assets she sold. She was pregnant with a child and she feared that her new born baby will not be healthy because she was not eating healthy food.

Leang managed to find a job as a gardener with the help of her friend Ekali. The salary was not much but at least it was worth doing it. But after a month, she couldn't work because of her pregnancy. So she took a leave of absence for a few months. Her boss was an understanding person and he didn't fire Leang but instead gave her advance payment and gave her maternity leave. Leang was happy because it was God who touched her employer's heart to show her some compassion. Leang knew that God really loved her and kept on hoping that everything will be fine.

As things were getting worst, she cried every single night thinking why her life was in such a bad situation. She missed her late husband and it was hard to erase the sweet memories out of her mind.

Thoughts often kept disturbing her mind. Promises and hopes were nothing but baffled words for her. Sometimes she felt that her husband broke his promises and left her alone. She knew that if she gives up then her children will be separated from her. Ekali was the only person she could talk to and share her problems with.

There was a shop in the colony in which Leang uses to take groceries for credit. After a few weeks, the retailer stopped giving her things on credit because Leang did not pay the due payment. She had no other source of income and her husband's pension was still not finalized and was taking a lot of time. Leang couldn't go to work, but she thought she can at least do something in her free time so she started knitting woolen sweaters, gloves and socks at home.

Her neighbors were rude to her and looked down on her family. She didn't blame her neighbors or even talked ill of them because it's how society is. She gave a deaf ear to the insults and critics.

Leang's two children stopped going to school because the principal told them not to attend the school classes unless their monthly fees are paid. Leang was helpless because at that moment they hardly had rice and food at home to feed her children. On knowing this, Ekali paid the school fees and told Leang that she can pay her back any day she can.

Life was very harsh on her but she still managed to keep the family together. She thought of selling the chickens she was rearing in the backyard of the house. But it was also stolen by her neighbors and she couldn't say a word. Besides her son, there was no man in the family and that's why the neighbors were taking advantage of their family.

After a few weeks, Leang went into labor. The weather was bad and it was windy and raining very heavily. Her daughter rushed to the phone booth and called Aunt Ekali.

When Ekali came to Leang's house, she was astonished to find no one in the room except her children. Leang was laid in the bed sweating and panting repeatedly. Ekali told the children to wait outside the room. Wasting no time she helped Leang deliver the newborn baby girl. Ekali called her husband to come and pick her up because it was already late at night. The first son told Aunt Ekali that none of the neighbors agreed to come. They didn't care to listen.

Ekali wept and wept thinking that Leang was really in a messed up situation but she still didn't show any signs of pain and regret. Ekali's husband came and took Leang to the hospital for better care and treatment. She was admitted in the hospital and stayed there for a few days. Ekali took good care of Leang's children and fed them well.

The next day, Leang's parents came to visit her. They were happy to see their newborn granddaughter but they also were worried as to how her daughter will manage to feed one more mouth. Her parents wanted to name the child but Leang refused in a very respectful and humble manner. It's a big issue for the tribal people in naming the newborn children. That's the reason I used the words respectful and humble.

Leang named her daughter Ekali. She told her friend, Ekali, that she is the only Good Samaritan and good friend she knows. On hearing that, Ekali was delighted of the respect she got from her friend. She never expected anything from Leang but when she named her child after her, Ekali was delighted.

After a month, Leang joined her old job. She would keep her baby in the cradle and would work. Her children didn't stop going to school. Very quickly she learned a lot about the business and taking care of the plants. She was not literate and could not read nor write. But she managed to learn hundreds of flowers and plants names.

After working for few months, she decided to start her own business as a florist and established small sector shops dealing with the sale of plants and flowers. She didn't find success at a blink of an eye but somehow her earnings were good.

Leang never re-married and remained a widow for the rest of her life. She even managed to convince the lady to whom she sold the piano to a few years back to sell it back to her and she paid double to get it back. Even if she could not buy her old house back, she was still happy living in a small rented house.

Leang's friend Ekali died of throat cancer after a few months. Before her death, Leang tended to her everyday and would encourage her to have faith to live longer. Ekali's last words to Leang were this, "My life on this earth is short but I am happy that I met a wonderful person like you."

Leang did not become very rich but she found herself contented with life. She was happy because she was earning money and feeding her children well. She never stopped going to church and paid a tenth for her tithes.

Friends should be few but of quality. Leang was strong enough to stand up and fight despite all the obstacles that stood in her way. Through this story, I would like to convey the message that despite all the temptations and trials in life, God still gives us a way to escape and overcome.

What if Leang had given up her children for adoption without putting up a fight to raise her own children? She wouldn't be as happy as she was after things became better. She always believed that God will fight for her and all she needed to do was to be still. Leang was a strong and independent woman who fought for her children and keeps her faith consolidated.

After ten years, Leang died from malaria. But before her death, she did so many good deeds for poor and needy widows. She led a good and full life. With every income and bonus in her business, she helped the poor by buying clothes and food for them. She would visit the orphans often and she was always willing to help the needy.

The faith of Sarah has been recorded in the book of Hebrews 11:11. And in the book of 1 Kings 17:21-24 it reads that Elijah the prophet cried out to the Lord and prayed that the child lives and the soul of the child returned. These women of faith were true believers of Christ. Leang never lost her faith in God and kept on moving forward. Faith is the substance of things hoped for the evidence of things not seen.

Chapter 5:

To Pull One

"Jesus beheld them, and said unto them, with men this is impossible but with God all things are possible." Matthew 19:26.

This is the story of a man who tried to overcome all his fears that stood in his way to success and he didn't give up pursuing success and happiness in his life even though it was very far from his reach.

The Life of Anyem

The story of Anyem is related to many strugglers in this world. But there are very few people that will fight their way to victory despite all the obstacles. Anyem was a man who kept on working hard in silence believing that he will achieve his goal one day.

Anyem was born to his parents in a small village in the hills. They were farmers and he had seven siblings, all of which were boys. Anyem's grandfather was a head hunter and there were lots of human skulls kept at home for memory.

There was no church in the village and there were very few Christians in the village but they were living a happy and contented life. The Christians in the village would gather on Sundays and have fellowship. Anyem's parents were not very religious but believed in God and were living an honest life. His parents made it mandatory for the family to attend the fellowship every Sunday. He loved attending the fellowships because every time he learned something new.

Anyem was good in playing football and running race but he was very different from his brothers and the other kids from his colony. His way of thinking and personality differed from other children. He was always eager to learn and he would spend most of his free time writing and drawing. His aim in life was to be a respected gazette officer in the society.

One day, when he was in the school, his mom came and got him while the classes were going on. It was harvest season and his parents wanted him to help them in the field. This was common in the village and it happened many times when he was attending school.

The education system was very deplorable and none of the villagers took education seriously. The parents would be more delighted when their children work in the fields and would know how to hunt wild animals. These were the qualities preferred over education in the village.

His hobbies were listening to radio every morning and playing football. His room was full of posters of politicians, musicians and sports stars. He loved writing down articles from old newspapers and magazines in his diary he maintained. The desire to learn and be more educated was driving him to an interesting life.

There was a teacher named Dumang in the village. He was married and was in his mid 40's. He had a dark complexion and was tall in height. Anyem would pay visit to his house often when he had free time to spare. He used to fetch water from the well for the teacher just to have a look at the world map and atlas book.

And sometimes he would mop the floor and clean it just to take some old newspapers to read. Anyem use to convince his teacher that he was doing all this work to show his appreciation towards him. That's the reason his teacher didn't stop him. Anyem would borrow books from his teacher and would read them at home. He wanted to buy a geometry box so he started saving every penny he got from his parents and relatives just to buy that.

There were only a few proud owners of television in the village. So on the weekends, all the neighbors would gather around to watch a movie in the house where there was a television. He was always excited to watch movies and music videos broadcasted. Sadly his family didn't own a television but he was satisfied with the radio his father bought. While watching movies and listening to the radio, he would always write down new facts, definitions and important news in his diary.

His work after school hours was to feed the pigs and go to the jungle to collect wood and eatable plants for the domestic animals in the house. Often he would use candles to study at night because some days the whole day he was busy playing or helping his mom in the kitchen. His village life was very interesting but he always felt that something was missing.

He wanted a better education and his environment would always discourage him. His parents managed to admit him in a private school in town area far from the village. His parents had full faith in him because he was a very hard working kid.

He lived with his uncle for two years and finished high school. During these two years, he had to walk three hours on foot to visit his parents in the village. While returning from home, he would carry a big bag of rice and red beans for his uncle and family. When his brothers visited him, they always brought vegetables and eatables from the field for him.

But there was a huge disappointment heading toward his family. Anyem was the first man from the village to finish matriculation. But there was a rich family from the village that claimed the title for their own son. It was a matter of pride and power in the village. Anyem's parents were helpless because in society only the rich takes control. It was a big insult to Anyem's family because there was nothing his family could do.

Anyem was not bothered that much because he knew that his life journey in achieving his goals has just began. He wanted to continue pursuing his studies but he wasted one year because his parents could not afford to send him to college. His parents sold the extra plot of land they owned and managed to send him to college. His parents made the choice to do so because they knew that their son will surely be a gazette officer in the future.

He was admitted in the hostel attached to the college in town area. Anyem was very innocent when he first entered college life. But his circle of friends was not good and he was introduced to many bad habits He started indulging himself in taking intoxicants and alcohol.

Anyem tried to adapt to life outside of the village. He was naughty but he was also very sincere in his studies. Anyem had very few good clothes and so most of the time he would wear the same shirt and jean pants. He kept long hair and also joined a music band. His favorite bands were "Smokie and CCR".

He didn't attend church on Sundays because he thought that even if he doesn't attend the church he had a clean heart. Anyem was having a good time in at the hostel but at the same time he never stopped studying hard. The desire to learn more and pursue success was always in his mind.

He and his circle of friends were also very naughty during college days. At one function in college, his circle of friends decided to play a prank on their lecturer. They kept a live lizard inside a shoe box and wrapped it with colorful plastic. At the function,

Anyem and his friends gifted the gift box and told the lecturer to open it in front of the attendants. When he opened the box, he found the lizard and started shouting loudly. The lecturer ran out of the room shouting help, help. For this Anyem and his friends were punished severely by the principal.

Often in the hostel kitchen, Anyem and his friends would go and eat the dish from the curry pot without anyone else noticing them. And after that they would fill the empty curry pot with charcoal and run. They did this many times but after a few months he and his friends were caught by the cook. The cook found a long hair on the curry pot. And Anyem was the only boy with long hair in the hostel. This was reported to the warden of the hostel. The warden got so angry and so he called Anyem and his friends in the office. The warden let them sign a paper with declaration that this is their last warning. But even this did not stop the circle of friends to be good students. While enjoying his life in the hostel and college, Anyem was forgetting that his parents were struggling to send him money monthly.

The one good quality about Anyem was that he never skipped a day without studying. He would visit the library very often and spend most of his time reading. At night when all of the boys were asleep, Anyem would wake up and study using a torch light.

One evening in the hostel, Anyem and his friends cooked dog meat and gave it to one of the hosteller who never had dog meat in his life. When that hosteller ate the meat, he was very happy. He was told that it was red meat and it was cooked well. After he finished eating the meat, Anyem and his friends told him that it was dog meat. He got very angry but at the same time could not say anything because he himself enjoyed the dog meat.

There was a week when the sweeper of the hostel didn't come to work. Anyem requested the warden pay him to do the cleaning. The warden didn't hesitate because he knew the condition of Anyem. He cleaned all the toilets and cleaned the mess hall as well. Anyem could not afford to buy text books and so he would borrow it from his friends or take from the library often.

After graduation, he applied for a job in a private office. He was paid well and he was able to send some of his monthly income to his parents. He was working hard and was supporting himself but he was not satisfied with that. He wanted to be a gazette officer and so he started to look for another job.

Finally, he managed to find a permanent job in a government office. He was working eight hours in a day unlike when he was working in a private office. After a few years passed, he was still not contented with his job. He felt empty and was not satisfied because he still didn't fulfill his dream.

His bad habits included drinking alcohol on a daily basis and he was a chain smoker. He started smoking during his college days but he didn't drink as much alcohol. But after college, he became an alcoholic because of the constant stress and problems he was facing.

He decided to take the competitive state exam. He could not enroll himself in the coaching centre because he was working in the office. So he studied after office hours and most nights he didn't sleep because he was studying very hard. After a few months, he took the state competitive exam but he didn't make it. But he didn't give up and continued studying.

Anyem took the exam the second time but he couldn't pass the second time as well. This time it was more discouraging for him because he knew some of his friends passed the exam. When his friends were driving a good car, living in a good house and enjoying the respect they got from society, Anyem was still preparing for the exam again. This discouraged him a lot but he didn't give up the idea of taking the exam again.

Finally, he passed the exam and became a gazette officer. He fulfilled his dream of finding success. He got married and God blessed his family with a son. He would not have found happiness in life if he had given up.

When he went back to his village, his family and friends greeted him. His parents were very happy and they killed a pig for celebration and invited all of the neighbors and fed them well and they were satisfied. He was like a celebrity in the village because of what he had become.

Later that evening, an elderly couple came to visit him. They came to apologize to Anyem for what they did. When Anyem passed his high school and became the first man from the village to pass matriculation, the title was snatched from him. Soon Anyem came to know who they were but he pretended as though nothing happened.

The elderly couple told Anyem that after doing what they did, none of their children passed metric exams and two of their children died of drug overdose. The curse of God was over their family. However, Anyem forgave them and told them that it does not matter anymore.

He went to meet his school teacher the next day. When he knocked at the door, the teacher's wife opened the door and invited him to the drawing room. She didn't recognize him but knew that Anyem was the little boy who visited her husband when he was a kid. He asked for her husband who was the teacher of Anyem.

Without saying a word, she went to the bedroom and brought a parcel for Anyem. She handed it to him and told her that her husband left it for Anyem before his death. As Anyem opened the parcel, there was an atlas text book and a letter. In the letter there was a simple message written. It read, "Congratulations Anyem, I knew that you would fulfill your dreams." On reading the note, Anyem started crying because he thought of all those days when he was a kid. His teacher had full faith in him that he would be successful in life. Anyem thanked his teacher's wife for keeping the parcel safe for him.

Things were better for Anyem compared to how his life was but he was still not contented. He had a beautiful unsuspecting wife, a good house and a son. When Anyem's parents visited him, they requested him to stop smoking and drinking alcohol because it would spoil the relationship with his wife. But he didn't listen to his parents. He had everything he wanted and there were no financial problems. He also managed to find good jobs for some of his siblings who were still in the village unemployed. But he felt something big was missing in his life.

He was not contented no matter how many times he tried to convince himself that he was successful because of his hard work. One negative habit about Anyem was that he took his friends advice seriously. Most of the time, he would quarrel over small issues because of this. Despite repeated request from his wife, Anyem was always taking advice from his friends.

One Sunday, he went to attend the church with his family. That Sunday the pastor was preaching the word of God based on the book of Romans 8:6 which read, "To be carnally minded is death: but to be spiritually minded is life and peace." This stroked his mind because this was exactly what he was looking for.

That same evening, Anyem had a discussion with his wife and he was telling his wife what was bothering him. Anyem wanted to leave his bad habits and live a good life. But it was very hard for him to stop drinking alcohol and smoking. Days passed by and he was trying hard. He decided to surrender his will to God and gave up his bad habits of smoking and addiction to alcohol.

The pastor made him a deacon in the church. Anyem was encouraged by 1 Peter 1:13 which read, "Wherefore grid up the lions of your mind, be sober, and hope to the end for the grace that is to be brought unto you at the revelation of Jesus Christ", whenever he felt like smoking again.

Whenever Anyem was at his weakest, he meditated on God's word and that kept him spiritually fit. He felt so satisfied and contended in life after accepting Jesus Christ as his savior. He finally found contentment in life. Philippians 4:13 says, "I can do all things through Christ which strengthened me."

Conclusion

The Bible teaches us to be very careful of how we think because our lives are shaped by our thoughts. Nothing shall separate us from the love of God if we only trust and obey. When you count your blessings one by one, you will see what God has done. The book of Proverbs also teaches us to guard our heart for everything we do flows from it. When you stop chasing after the wrong things, you will definitely give the right things a chance to catch you. Always be thankful and think about how rich you are because your family you have is priceless and your time on earth is gold. God is our treasure and He will never fail nor forsake you.

Index

Chapter 1: Cast Forth - The Life of Longshi

Bible references:

1. Romans 8:18
2. 1 Timothy 6:10
3. Philippians 1:6

Points to be noted:

A. Contentment is a skill and it does not just come to you.

B. The love of money is the root of all evil.

C. Money exercises power over us and it blinds you to the power it has. Money is very different from other things, materialism and greed is a sin of the sin.

D. Spiritual depression is caused by sin. God occasionally permits it to come upon us that we may know ourselves and feel our own weakness.

E. God is the omnipresent, omnipotent and omniscient. He is our creator, sustainer and guardian and provider and protector.

Chapter 2: A Dark Horse - The Life of Soren

Bible references:

1. Proverbs 16:9

2. Luke 7: 12-16

Points to be noted:

A. Strong belief in the doctrine of religion based on spiritual conviction rather than proof.

B. Don't let fear that you will be a burden to others.

C. Overcome the fear of death or dying by looking forward to heaven.

D. A man's heart deviseth his way but the Lord directed his steps.

E. God knows what's best for us and will give us what we need in the right time.

F. Overcome the fear of death and dying by looking forward to heaven.

Chapter 3: On the Rack - The Worship Leader

Bible references:

1. Matthew 6:5

2. Jonah 1-4

Points to remember:

    A.   God will judge you.

    B.   Vain and useless discourses are a great burden to the spiritual growth and especially to a weary spiritual mind that needs betterment.

    C.   Teachers may teach the doctrine, true and useful but without putting it to action it is dead. That's when Satan may abuse and pervert scripture.

Chapter 4: The Evening of Life - Leang's Life

Bible references:

1. Proverbs 15:3
2. Hebrews 11:11
3. 1 Kings 17: 21-24

Points to remember:

    A.   The eye of the Lord is everywhere.

    B.   Be remembered for good.

    C.   Faith is the substance of things hoped for the evidence of things not seen

Chapter 5: To Pull One -The Life of Anyem

Bible references:

1. Matthew 19:26
2. Romans 8:6
3. 1 Peter 1:13
4. Philippians 4:13

Points to remember:

A. To be carnally minded is death: but to be spiritually minded is life and peace.
B. I can do all things through Christ which strengthened me.

Ordinary Nagas With Exceptional Stories

www.ingramcontent.com/pod-product-compliance
Lightning Source LLC
Chambersburg PA
CBHW050044080526
44586CB00014B/1446